LOUDER THAN WORDS

Jill Posener was born in and lives in London. She grew up in Malaysia and Berlin. After school she trained and worked as a stage manager. She wrote Gay Sweatshop Theatre Company's first women's play, *Any Woman Can*, performed first in 1976. She stayed with the company for two years.

She managed the women's rock band The Mistakes until their sad demise in 1981, when she started taking photography seriously. Her first book, *Spray It Loud*, was first published in 1982, and reprinted in 1986.

Jill Posener served as an adviser to the Community Arts Sub-committee of the Greater London Council, which was abolished by Thatcher's government in 1986.

In 1985 Jill Posener visited Australia and it is from this visit that the Australian content of *Louder Than Words* comes.

She lives with Clara the cat and a friend, and dreams of the Australian bush.

JILL POSENER
LOUDER THAN WORDS

London and New York

First published in 1986 by
Pandora Press
(Routledge & Kegan Paul plc)
11 New Fetter Lane, London EC4P 4EE
Published in the USA by
Routledge & Kegan Paul Inc.
in association with Methuen Inc.
29 West 35th Street, New York, NY 10001
Set in Franklin Gothic
by Foremost Typesetting Ltd, London SE1 0LH
and printed in Great Britain
by Butler & Tanner Ltd, Frome and London
Designed by Angela Stewart Park
© Jill Posener 1986

Library of Congress Cataloging in Publication Data

Posener, Jill
Louder than words

Graffiti—Australia.   2. Feminism—Australia.
I. Title.
GT3913.89.A2P67   1986   082   86-5074

British Library CIP Data also available

ISBN 0-86358-086-6

● For My Mum Charmian. And for Bonzo, Clara and Suzy Hoo with love

London 1983

BUGA UP Australia

Contents

Melbourne 1985

Acknowledgments

The author would like to thank: Sue O'Sullivan and Suzy Houligan for everything.
Suzy Fielding.
Jan Bradshaw for the title.
All the girls in Melbourne: Fran · Sue · Mitch · Barb · Merle · Sara · Sandra · Margie · Trudy
Sue · Jan · Gail · Sybylla Press and especially Deborah Kelly for graphics.
David Thompson in Sydney and Mary and Jules in Adelaide.
Penny · Jo · Jenny · And all those in London: Jane · Sybil · Penny · Helen · Berta · Kate · Lisa.
Special thanks to dear Danielle, to Linda for some astute editing and to precious Cheryl. You
too Roy.

BUGA UP (Billboard Utilising Graffitists Against Unhealthy Promotions) in Melbourne and
Sydney took time to show me their work and share it with me. I am deeply grateful to Marg
White in Melbourne and Peter in Sydney. Their energy and creativity is an inspiration.

COUGH UP (Citizens' Organisation Using Graffiti to Halt Unhealthy Promotions) and COUGH IN
(Campaign On Use of Graffiti for Health in Neighbourhoods) keep up the good work in the UK.
Thanks to Grove Hardy Ltd for photographic printing. Also to the Women's Press in London who
publish the postcards. Don Mathew spent time telling me about Friends of the Earth's sticker
campaign. Thanks too to Becky, Stephanie and to Sarah Tisdall.

Thanks to BUGA UP for the photos on pages VI and 5 and Cath Tate for the photo on page 16 and
Suzy Fielding for the photo on page 24 and Jeremy Iles for the photo on page 70. And finally,
though there's little graffiti in the paradise of North East Victoria, I'm grateful to Dee and Euni in
Mhyree, and to Ute, Jenny, Golom, the dogs and cattle at Sandy Creek and to Joycie and Ellie at
Granya for the many hours of bliss I spent in your homes and on your land.

To all the graffitists . . . sprayed from the heart.

Melbourne 1985

This second graffiti book continues my support for the graffitists. They take all the risks. Mine is the easy part. A casual Sunday outing in the car, camera by my side, turning the corner and the sudden sight of spray paint all over a sexist ad. My pulse quickens, my heart leaps, I leap — out of the car that is — and capture another addition to our walls. For me, all the paint, all the slogans, remind me that we are fighting back.

My fury about the use of sexist imagery remains unabated over the years. The continuous use of our bodies to sell products should be outlawed, especially as the use of young women and girls on ads seems to be increasing. It's past time the advertisers took our bodies off their hoardings. A range of products from toys to contraceptives, cars and alcohol use women in a gratuitously offensive way. They use the blatant sexism which some men find so amusing and which women are affronted and outraged by. Many of us now carry our spray cans along with our front door keys and diaries.

Cigarette advertising has also been a graffiti target for a long time. In Australia BUGA UP and in the UK COUGH UP and COUGH IN have been increasingly busy. Every year around 100,000 people die in the UK from smoking-related deaths. For a product which causes so many preventable deaths the cigarette manufacturers are very bold in their advertising.

The same is true of car manufacturers whose advertising style has become more daring as the market becomes ever more competitive. Suggesting that a car can easily exceed the speed limit by using slogans like 'The trigger under your foot' or 'Even with the speedo at 120mph it's quiet. You don't realise you're going so fast' is irresponsible at best.

Quite simply, products which maim, kill and destroy have no place in the advertising of any country. So, where is the strong arm of the Advertising Standards Authority, the self-policing body who claim to clamp down on ads which aren't 'Decent Legal Honest'? Their laughable claim has been exposed over and over again by complainants to the Authority and by graffitists who have long been an alternative voice to the ad industry.

Cigarettes may be legal, but that doesn't make them decent or the marketing of them honest in any way. And why does the ASA condone the breach of the law which advertisers are suggesting when they emphasise a car's capability to break the speed limit, as opposed to its capability to brake in fog on the M25?

But anger and frustration aren't the only reasons I spend my days searching the streets. Sometimes graffiti makes me laugh out loud. But the writing and drawings on the walls are temporary in their original setting. I document them because they are part of our struggle. As photographs they survive, they inform and they link together.

Whether it's the anger against domestic violence in London or the cheeky humour of the graphic artists in Melbourne, they are all redecorating and retaking the patriarchal streets.

It's honest writing for a change.

A Woman's Touch

> " I started doing graffiti as an alternative to blowing things up. About a year ago I began to wonder what could be done about the Pregnancy Problem Action Centre, a Right to Life front, which tells young women terrifying lies about abortion. I decided that bombing them would just make them feel more righteous and martyred, give them more ammunition in their 'holy war'. Without their financial power and access to the media, graffiti seemed like an appropriate way to shriek defiance at them. "

Graffitist, Melbourne

London 1983

London 1983

BUGA UP Australia

> **The streets are public places. Graffiti is an expression of the experiences and ideas of people who live on those streets, but don't own them or the houses or the businesses. Graffiti creates solidarity between all those people. It isn't academic, it's immediate and doesn't require money. I like watching reactions to my graffiti. Is it painted over, or added to? Sometimes the reactions make me think again, maybe add something else. It's like asking questions.**
>
> **One graffiti I did was on a church wall. I put 'Isn't your God a Misogynist?' It helped break one of my own taboos, while expressing my anger at religion. It felt good.**

Graffitist, Melbourne

Melbourne 1985

Melbourne 1985

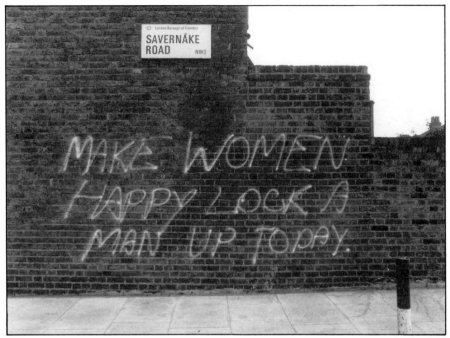

London 1983

Melbourne 1985

Melbourne 1985

Melbourne 1985

Melbourne 1985

Melbourne 1985

While the media coined the phrase 'post feminism' and deliberately turned its back on the 'ugly and aggressive' or 'wild and woolly' stereotypes it had created for the women's movement, the words coming from the movement itself and from the spray cans of women are very much 'feminism now'.

Graffitists remind us that despite all the legislation in the world, and with the supposed benefits of a new role sharing society, women are as vulnerable to sexual violence as ever. Rape, sexual assault and murder of women and girls are on the increase.

As the tabloids and so-called quality papers tire of Greenham baiting and want to find a new toy, the radical women's movement and graffitists remain the only agitators for a safe world for women. Men haven't made the changes.

Melbourne 1985

London 1985

London 1984

London 1985

The sinking of the ship Rainbow Warrior by the French secret service in Auckland Harbour in 1985, brought the name Greenpeace to a world audience. The anti-nuclear and conservation group has been one of the most effective exponents of direct action in campaigns to halt the destruction of our natural resources.

But all of that does not make their 1985 ad campaign any more palatable.

'It is hugely offensive in many ways. In the way the model, with her slit skirt, is made to stand as though she were posing for a pornographic magazine. In the use of the word "dumb", implying women's stupidity while offending those without speech who oppose the use of the word dumb to describe their disability for exactly that reason, that it suggests idiocy.

And, above all, it ignores the role of men who control the profits and the killing of the fur trade. Greenpeace shouldn't have produced slick sexism in its opposition to a bloody trade.'

Annie Razor (rubbing out nasty advertising)

Neither should the Body Shop, whose range of natural beauty products sell primarily to women, have sponsored some of the advertising sites.

London 1985

Cath Tate, London

London 1985

London 1983

London 1985

London 1983

Melbourne 1985

London 1985

'The Campaign for the Feminine Woman regards Women's Lib as a dangerous cancer and a perversion in human society which must be eradicated.'

A statement from the Campaign's publicity handout

The Campaign, founded by Mr David Stait, encourages its members to hold coffee mornings to 'propagate' and 'promote the virtue of femininity in the female'. So, all across the shires of this green and pleasant land fearful supporters are discussing the 'sinister purpose' of women's liberation and persuading disbelievers that after all 'the male has a larger brain'.

London 1985

London 1985

London 1985

London 1983

Melbourne 1985

Melbourne 1985

Sue Felding, Melbourne

London 1985

Sydney 1985

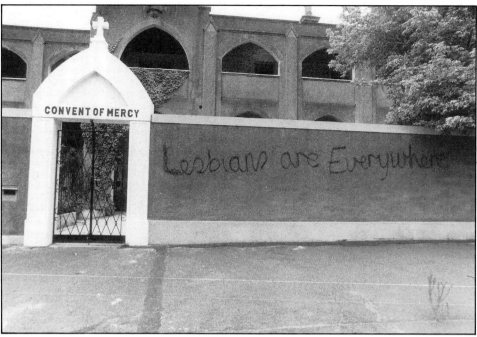

Melbourne 1985

'See the Nun! That used to be me. How strange to see one so self-contained, untouchable, other worldly. Are we looking at me? (God calls only a few. We know not why he chooses us from amongst our companions. He has given us the greatest privilege of all, a call to religious life.)

See the Lesbian? That looks like me. How tense she stands, as though ready to spring for a quick exit. After all, many in this crowd view her as a sinner, abomination, one who is dangerous to little girls. Do you suppose Jesus would wash her feet?

How could I appear so Madonna-like to some? So approved? So whore-like to others? So disapproved? I never planned to be unusual.'

Wendy Sequoia, ex nun. From Lesbian Nuns: Breaking Silence, *edited by Rosemary Curb and Nancy Manahan, Naiad Press, 1985, Tallahassee, Florida, reproduced by kind permission of the publisher*

Melbourne 1985

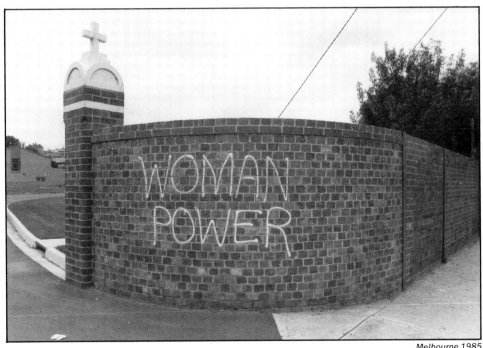

Melbourne 1985

London 1983

Widows was a successful television series notable for its portrayal of four strong women characters. The women, bereaved when their husbands die during a dangerous robbery, decide to carry out the raid themselves, and succeed. Led by Dolly, the eldest and most sympathetic character, they make an amazing escape with the money. This graffiti appeared the week the series ended.

Amsterdam 1982

Amsterdam 1982

London 1982

Strength and dignity are her clothing;
And she laugheth at the time to come.
She openeth her mouth with wisdom;
And the law of kindness is on her tongue. "

Proverbs 31: 25-6

Amsterdam 1982

" *If people want to make war they should make a colour war and paint each other's cities up in the night in pinks and greens.* **"**

Yoko Ono

" *Today we have done what we had to do. If necessary we will do it again. We Americans are slow to anger. We always seek peaceful avenues before resorting to the use of force.* **"**

Ronald Reagan

Ronald Rambo Reagan after bombing Tripoli and Benghazi causing civilian casualties on April 14 1986

Vietnam, Korea, Cambodia, Grenada, Nicaragua, Cuba, Chile. We must have imagined it all.

Sydney 1985

Melbourne 1985

Melbourne 1985

Melbourne 1985

Vietnam has always been seen as America's war. But in the late 1950s Australia's government, led by Menzies, was paranoid about supposed Chinese communist expansion in South East Asia. This led to Australia's direct involvement in the Vietnam war.

At the peak of military activity there were 910,000 foreign troops on Vietnamese soil. A total of 46,852 Australian troops served in Vietnam: 494 were killed and a further 2,398 injured.

Whitlam's Labour government finally withdrew troops and aid in 1972, ten years after the first personnel arrived in Vietnam. Public opinion had been steadily moving towards withdrawal and throughout the war there had been a strong, radical anti-war and anti-conscription movement.

Australian soldiers gained a reputation as 'tough jungle fighters' who hated everybody, especially the Vietnamese. A leaflet, put out by some soldiers as they left Vietnam called 'Advice on the Rehabilitation of a Soldier', made the following suggestions:

'Get the women off the streets, hide the grog, chain the fridge, lock the cow in the barn' because

'He's no longer the sweet-tempered angel he was when he left Australia. He has to become reaccustomed to blond and respectable women, civilian manners and ordinary food.'

Source for figures: Australia's Vietnam, *ed. Peter King, Allen & Unwin, 1983*

Melbourne 1985

London 1983

Pine Gap is situated near the red centre of Australia, 12 miles south west of Alice Springs.

It is one of three major US military bases on Australian soil, and is one of the most sophisticated communications centres in the world. The functions of Pine Gap are shrouded in mystery, but like women at Greenham Common, at Comiso in Sicily and others in Holland and Germany, Australian women have broken the silence about American military bases around the world.

In addition to the very real threat of having a foreign superpower on Australian land, Pine Gap is Aboriginal land, an ancient and sacred site, a place for women's 'dreaming' rituals. Stop Pine Gap.

Adelaide 1985

Melbourne 1985

Melbourne 1985

Melbourne 1985

" A rose is a rose is a rose
loveliness extreme
sweetest ice cream "

From Sacred Emily *by Gertrude Stein*

London 1983

London 1985

The Hibakusha — the Japanese term for nuclear victims — demand that there be 'No More Hiroshimas, No More Nagasakis'. The bombs fell on 6 and 9 August 1945. In the first four months the death toll was between 130-140,000 in Hiroshima and between 60-70,000 in Nagasaki. The cities were totally destroyed. Those people near the centre of the blast were incinerated, literally became nothing. Where there were people before, there were just shadows on the ground.

London 1985

London 1985

London 1984

" *Originally the idea was to dismantle the display; we hadn't thought of painting the slogans. But when we climbed up, there was a pot of black gloss and a brush just lying there. Seemed a shame to waste it.*

We walked along Whitehall with a long ladder, propped it up against the theatre and climbed onto the building and began pulling the display to bits, stamping on the models of soldiers and tanks.

We threw ticker tape with women's symbols on it and shouted to let passersby know what we were doing and why. The painting really was an afterthought. Funny really. Lots of tourists smiled, especially Japanese. They were pleased to see our action. The police arrived within ten minutes. We were all arrested and later convicted of criminal damage and obstruction and fined £290 each, and given conditional discharges.

Graffiti is great. It's some honest writing for a change. **"**

Becky

Eight women, who had met through their involvement with Greenham Common, were outraged at the blatant militarism of a Theatre of War in Central London, but also by the fact that the theatre owner was porn king Paul Raymond. Sex and war, linked financially and politically, both controlled by men and with most of us caught in the crossfire.

London 1983

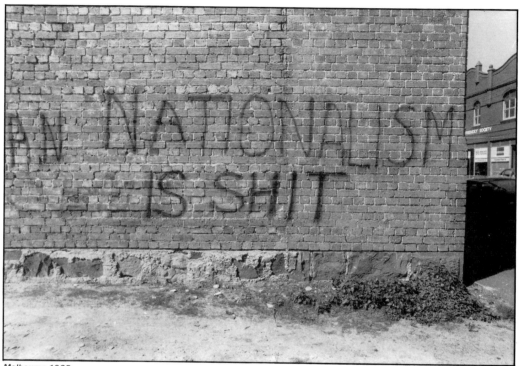

Melbourne 1985

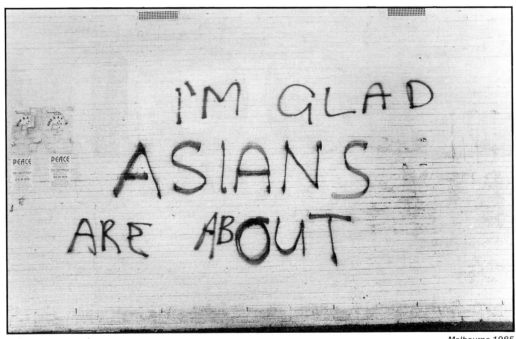

Melbourne 1985

Melbourne 1985

London 1985

London 1983

London 1983

Melbourne 1985

" **For us it is a question of crushing fascism once and for all. Yes, and in spite of government.**

No government in the world fights fascism to the death. When the bourgeoisie sees power slipping from its grasp it has recourse to fascism to maintain itself.

You never can tell, you know — the government might yet need these forces to crush the workers' movement. We (the workers) are going to inherit the earth. There is not the slightest doubt about that. The bourgeoisie might blast and ruin its own world before it leaves the stage of history. We are not in the least afraid of ruins. We, the workers, can build to take their place. We carry a new world here in our hearts. **"**

Buenaventura Durutti, Spanish Anarchist, 1896-1936

London 1984

London 1983

Melbourne 1985

London 1985

London 1984

London 1985

London 1985

London 1984

Graffiti, like the huge Free George Davis ones in East London, often last longer than the events that inspire them. Sarah Tisdall says:

 Being the subject of graffiti is a strange feeling, like it is really about someone else, not about me. The graffiti wasn't for me, it was aimed at the Guardian, but it's moving that someone felt strongly enough to do it. Funny though, they spelt my name right and got the Guardian wrong. The press usually got it the other way round. "

On Friday 21 October 1983 two photocopied documents, classified 'Secret-UK eyes A', and written by Defence Secretary Michael Heseltine, arrived at the *Guardian* newspaper. They were sent anonymously. The memorandum concerned the date of arrival of Cruise missiles in Britain and the government's public relations plan around the arrival. With CND enjoying renewed popularity and Greenham Common Women's Peace Camp gaining huge public support, the government was scared of outraged public opinion on the issue.

Melbourne 1985

The arrival date was published on 22 October and the content of the public relations memo on 31 October. Immediately a leaks inquiry was set in motion. The *Sun* newspaper described the leaker of the documents as 'a treacherous mole' and asked 'Is there not a danger that out of some twisted political convictions, *he* is prepared to betray us all to a potential enemy?'

The *Guardian* effectively led the inquiry to Sarah Tisdall, the 23-year-old clerk in the Foreign Office, by returning the documents.

Sarah Tisdall was suspended from duty on 9 January 1984 and charged under the Official Secrets Act. She was sentenced to six months' imprisonment.

Had the newspaper destroyed the documents, Sarah Tisdall might well have continued her quiet and uneventful life in the Civil Service.

Asked whether she was opposed to nuclear weapons she answered that she was not, but that 'I felt the public had a right to know what was being done to them. I am not a spy, but I could not sit there and just let them go through with it because I felt it was immoral.'

“ *Graffiti cheers me up. I've often laughed at it and felt that I'm not alone, and that's important for our emotional survival. It's good fun and the adrenalin buzz is good for me. I like the challenge of having a safe time, a limited time to decide what I want to say. I like the fun of mucking it up completely and it not being the end of the world, just funny. I love doing colourful ones because colour is good for the eyes and I love the texture of spray paint.* **”**

Graffitist, Melbourne

Melbourne 1985

Melbourne 1985

Melbourne 1985

Sydney 1985

Melbourne 1985

Melbourne 1985

Sydney 1985

" *I think graffiti could be called exhibitionist. I like that word especially relating to graffiti drawings because I like drawings to be outside gallery exhibitions. With writing, it's a boisterous way of expressing things which people can't avoid seeing. Graffiti has to be big because otherwise we just remain silent in the environment of the fatherland.* **"**

Graffitist, Melbourne

London 1983

Sydney 1985

London 1985

Melbourne 1985

London 1983

London 1985

London 1985

London 1985

Hampshire 1983

Jeremy Iles, London

Friends of the Earth Transport Campaigner Don Mathew decided, after a fruitless correspondence with the ASA and the advertisers, to use a different tactic. After six months of letter-writing Don felt driven to direct action because all else had failed.

Emphasising the beneficial effect of humour, he produced one of the most inspired redecoration campaigns. Ready printed, sticky cut-outs of the grim reaper were stuck behind the steering wheel on the ads and huge Speed Kills banners were stuck across the bottom of the hoardings.

When the ad agency discovered which poster site was going to be re-faced, they hurriedly covered the entire poster in brown paper. Their attitude seemd to be: 'If you're going to ruin our advert, we'd rather do it first!'

'More like a bullet than a bullet'

Toyota sell a lot of cars. Presumably they are reliable and safe and all the other 'good' things a car should be. I don't think that a car's resemblance to a deadly weapon makes good advertising copy. But the above sentence is a sales slogan for a Toyota car. So is 'The Trigger Under Your Foot'. Compare those to the Code of Practice from the Advertising Standards Authority: 'Advertisements should neither condone anti-social or violent behaviour.' Of course there's nothing anti-social or violent about guns and bullets.

The ASA states that it doesn't mind advertisers emphasising the capability of a car to exceed the speed limit, as long as there is no undue emphasis placed on actually driving at such speeds. So, why didn't they mind when Astra advertised its hatchback with 'Even with the speedo at 120mph it's quiet. You don't realise you're going so fast.' Or the Cavalier SRi with 'What a wonderfully easy car to drive fast'.

Melbourne 1985

❝ *Smoking is a shocking thing — blowing smoke out of our mouths into other people's mouths, eyes and noses, and having the same thing done to us.* **❞**

Samuel Johnson (not known for particularly enlightened views on other matters), 1773

London 1983

The smoker

The passive smoker

The smoker inhales mainstream smoke which contains a treacly tar (which irritates the lungs and can cause cancer), carbon monoxide (which starves the body of oxygen and may lead to heart attacks), and nicotine (a very addictive poison) plus a variety of other gases and poisons.

The passive smoker breathes in sidestream smoke, diluted in the air. This is unfiltered smoke, and contains higher concentrations of the poisonous chemicals and gases than mainstream smoke. It contains twice as much nicotine, 3 times as much tar, 5 times as much carbon monoxide 50 times as much cancer causing chemicals

London 1983

London 1985

London 1984

London 1982

London 1983

Melbourne 1985

In Australia two cigarette manufacturers suffered marketing blows in 1985.

Two successful motor racing teams failed to renew their sponsorship deals with Philip Morris (producers of Marlboro) and Rothmans (producers of Peter Stuyvesant). After initially denying that public opinion against smoking had anything to do with their decisions, both teams admitted that the generally unfavourable public attitude to cigarette advertising was a crucial factor in the change.

One driver says 'I feel easier not wearing Marlboro logos.'

go for it !

Sydney 1985

Melbourne 1985

Melbourne 1985

> **Advertisements now appear as part of nearly all mass communication in the form of television, radio and print media as well as featuring ever more frequently in everyday life in the form of packaging, billboards, point of sale advertising. After the United States and South Africa, Australia is the third most advertising saturated country in the world.**
>
> **BUGA UP started spontaneously a few years ago with a small group of people who decided to retaliate against this domination by advertising. By refacing billboards BUGA UP turns the one-way communication of advertising into a two-way interchange of images and ideas.**

From Adexpo. A Self-defence Course for Children *by BUGA UP*

London 1984

London 1985

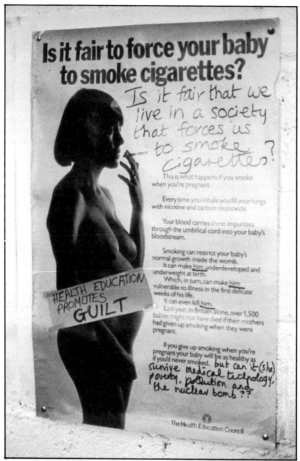

London 1982

Smoking is a political issue. The tobacco industry is amongst the most exploitative in its conditions and payments to workers on the plantations and in the factories. Governments are not inclined to clean up an industry which provides billions in taxes and while MPs have conflicting interests as directors of tobacco companies, how can we expect legislation about the marketing and sale of cigarettes and tobacco?

Most tobacco companies are heavily involved in South Africa. Perhaps, while the radical left and the Women's Movement are demanding the boycotting of South African goods, they should take a look at the cigarette they're puffing away on. For example, Rothmans International, based in Britain but controlled from South Africa, markets the brands Rothmans, Dunhill and Peter Stuyvesant.

London 1985

Remember, if you ever feel the urge to use a spray can on a hoarding or a wall, that you are committing an offence. If caught in the act, there is little you can do except get immediate legal advice and help. Inform someone in advance that you intend to go spray painting and carry a solicitor's phone number with you. You will be charged with criminal damage and fines can be heavy. Imprisonment is unlikely, but possible in serious cases.

Buga Up: Box 80, Strawberry Hills
N.S.W. 2012,
Australia.

Melbourne 1985

Sydney 1985

HA HA HA
HE ME HE
I'M THE
PHAMTON
SCRIBBLER
AND YOU CANT
CATCH ME.